The AIDS Awareness Library™

Heroes Against AIDS

Anna Forbes, MSS

The Rosen Publishing Group's

New York

Published in 1996 by The Rosen Publishing Group, Inc.
29 East 21st Street, New York, NY 10010

First Edition

Book design: Erin McKenna

Photo credits: Cover © AP/Wide World Photos; pp. 4, 12, 15 by Guillermina DeFerrari; p. 7 © Shock Photography/Liaison International; p. 8 © Jim Bourg/The Gamma Liaison Network; p. 11 © Doug Vann/Photoreporters; p. 16 © Markel/Liaison; p. 19 by Sarah Friedman; p. 20 © Allan Clear/Impact Visuals.

Manufactured in the United States of America

Contents

A Disease Called AIDS

AIDS is a disease that is spreading all over the world. Half a million people in the United States have AIDS. About one million people have HIV, the **virus** (VY-rus) that causes AIDS. The two most common ways people get HIV are by having unsafe sex or by sharing needles to use drugs.

HIV takes about ten years to become AIDS.

Most people with HIV can do the same things as people without HIV. It takes a long time for HIV to become AIDS.

The Fight Against AIDS

Lots of people are fighting AIDS. Some of them have AIDS and some don't. Some people are paid to do AIDS work. Others are **volunteers** (vol-un-TEERZ). Doctors and nurses help people with AIDS stay as healthy as possible. Scientists and researchers are looking for a cure for AIDS. Teachers and performers help people learn more about AIDS. Writers write about AIDS. This book tells you about some of the other ways people are fighting AIDS.

Scientists are working hard to find a cure for AIDS. ▶

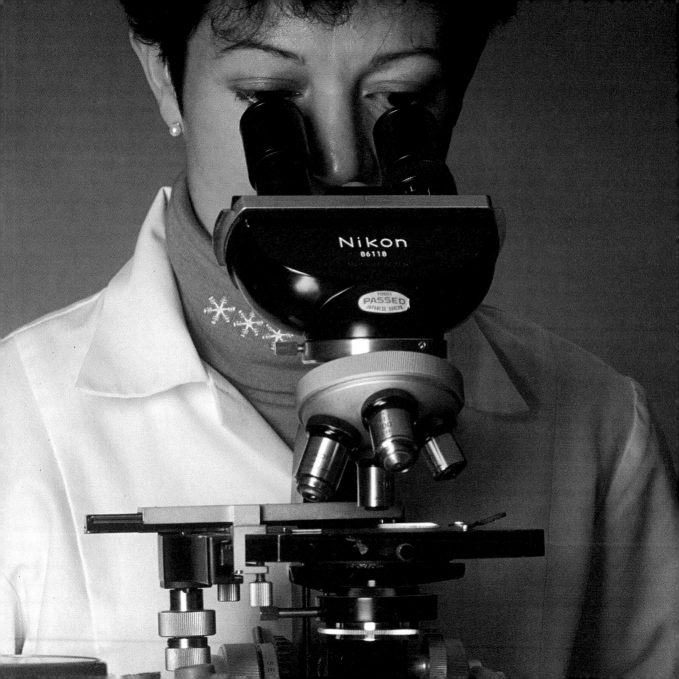

Famous People Fighting AIDS

In 1992, basketball star Magic Johnson found out that he had HIV. He stopped playing basketball and taught kids about AIDS. He visited schools and youth programs, telling kids how to stay safe from AIDS.

Magic decided that having HIV wasn't going to stop him from doing what he loved best. He began playing basketball again. By doing that, he showed the whole world that people with HIV can do many of the same things as people who don't have HIV.

◀ Magic Johnson is helping people understand the facts about HIV by talking about his experiences with it.

Kids Fighting AIDS

At the age of 13, Ryan White was thrown out of school because he had AIDS. He and his family fought in court for his right to go to school. Two years later, the courts decided that he, and every kid with HIV or AIDS, had the right to go to school. People all over the United States came to learn the facts about HIV and AIDS because of Ryan's struggle. Ryan died when he was 18. By that time, Ryan had helped change the laws that would affect thousands of kids with HIV or AIDS.

Thanks to Ryan White, kids with HIV or AIDS are now allowed to go school. ▶

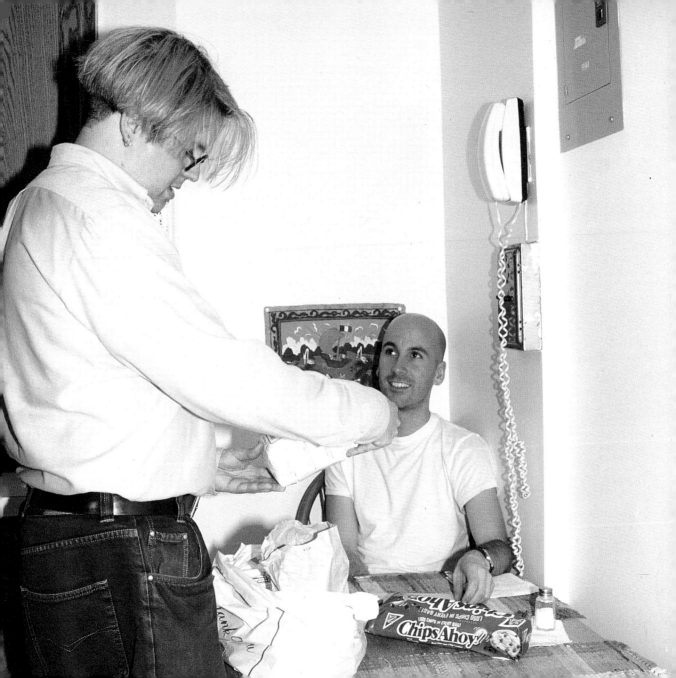

Glenn

AIDS Buddies

AIDS Buddy volunteers help people with AIDS in everyday ways. Glenn is Jeff's AIDS Buddy. Jeff has AIDS. When Jeff feels tired or sick, Glenn can help him by shopping for food and doing his laundry. Glenn also helps by spending time with Jeff. Glenn is Jeff's friend. They watch TV or play cards or just talk. Glenn helps make Jeff's life easier and more fun.

All it takes to be an AIDS Buddy is the desire to help someone.

◀ An AIDS Buddy helps make life a little easier and more fun for a person who has AIDS.

Counselors

Judith is an AIDS **counselor** (KOWN-sel-er). AIDS counselors help people with AIDS get things like food, clothes, money for medicine, and a safe place to live.

Judith also runs a **support** (suh-PORT) group for teens with AIDS. At the group meetings, the kids share their feelings about having AIDS. Sometimes they feel scared, and sometimes they feel sad. No matter how someone feels, it helps to talk about it. Judith helps them deal with their feelings.

An AIDS counselor helps people share their feelings about having the disease. ▶

Fundraisers

Eric is a **fundraiser** (FUND-ray-zer). That means that he raises money to help fight AIDS. Eric gets thousands of people to join the AIDS Walk every year. The AIDS Walk is an event that raises money to give to places that help people with AIDS. People who do the AIDS Walk get money from their friends, family, and neighbors for every mile they walk. Last year, Eric's AIDS Walk raised over a million dollars for the fight against AIDS.

◀ Many people can take part in fundraising events such as the AIDS Walk.

Epidemiologists

Ruth is an **epidemiologist** (EP-ih-dee-mee-OLL-eh-jist). She studies **epidemics** (ep-ih-DEM-iks). An epidemic is a disease that spreads to a lot of people very quickly. AIDS is an epidemic. Ruth keeps track of every-thing about the AIDS epidemic in her city. For example, she finds out how many people have AIDS and how they got it. Ruth's work helps us learn more about how to stop AIDS from spreading. It also tells us what kinds of help people with AIDS need.

18

An epidemiologist finds out how many people have AIDS and how they got it. ▶

Vivian

Activists

Vivian is an **activist** (AK-ti-vist). Activists point out problems and get people to work together to help solve them. Vivian has AIDS. She helps mothers with AIDS take care of their children. Vivian got several people to help her set up Vivian's Place. Vivian's Place is a house where women with AIDS and their kids can live. The moms get help taking care of their kids. And the kids get to live with other kids going through the same things as they are.

◀ Another kind of activist is someone who participates in protests and marches in support of the fight against AIDS.

You Can Be a Hero Too

Lots of people are helping to fight HIV and AIDS. There are many ways you can help too. You can learn how to stay safe from AIDS by not having sex and not sharing needles or using drugs. You can talk to your friends and family about AIDS. You can also teach others not to be afraid of people with HIV or AIDS.

The fight against AIDS is huge and important. Everyone who fights AIDS is a hero.

22

Glossary

activist (AK-ti-vist) Person who points out problems and works to solve them.

counselor (KOWN-sel-er) Person who helps others.

epidemic (ep-ih-DEM-ik) The quick spread of a disease.

epidemiologist (EP-ih-dee-mee-OLL-eh-jist) Person who tracks epidemics.

fundraiser (FUND-ray-zer) Person who raises money.

support (suh-PORT) To help or offer comfort.

virus (VY-rus) Germ that causes disease.

volunteer (vol-un-TEER) To work without pay.

Index